Cadaver Dog

www.lukebest.me

Luke Best was born in Toowoomba, where he lives and works. His poetry has been published in literary journals including *Overland, Verity La, Stilts Journal, Concrescence, Mascara Literary Review* and *Tincture Journal*. His manuscript *Percussion* was Highly Commended in the 2017 Thomas Shapcott Prize. *Cadaver Dog* is Luke's first book and won the 2019 Thomas Shapcott Prize.

THE ARTS QUEENSLAND THOMAS SHAPCOTT POETRY PRIZE SERIES

Lidija Cvetkovic *War Is Not the Season for Figs*
Jaya Savige *latecomers*
Nathan Shepherdson *Sweeping the Light Back into the Mirror*
Angela Gardner *Parts of Speech*
Sarah Holland-Batt *Aria*
Felicity Plunkett *Vanishing Point*
Rosanna Licari *An Absence of Saints*
Vlanes *Another Babylon*
Nicholas Powell *Water Mirrors*
Rachael Briggs *Free Logic*
David Stavanger *The Special*
Krissy Kneen *Eating My Grandmother: a grief cycle*
Stuart Barnes *Glasshouses*
Shastra Deo *The Agonist*
Rae White *Milk Teeth*
Anna Jacobson *Amnesia Findings*

Luke **Best**

Cadaver Dog

UQP

First published 2020 by University of Queensland Press
PO Box 6042, St Lucia, Queensland 4067 Australia

uqp.com.au
reception@uqp.uq.edu.au

Copyright © Luke Best 2020
The moral rights of the author have been asserted.

This book is copyright. Except for private study, research, criticism or reviews, as permitted under the *Copyright Act*, no part of this book may be reproduced, stored in a retrieval system, or transmitted in any form or by any means without prior written permission. Enquiries should be made to the publisher.

Cover design by Sandy Cull, www.sandycull.com
Author photograph by Sarah Gage Photography
Typeset in 11.5/15 pt Bembo Std by Post Pre-press Group, Brisbane
Printed in Australia by McPherson's Printing Group

 This project is supported by the Queensland Government through Arts Queensland.

  The University of Queensland Press is assisted by the Australian Government through the Australia Council, its arts funding and advisory body.

Scripture quotations taken from *The Holy Bible*, New International Version® NIV® Copyright © 1973 1978 1984 2011 by Biblica, Inc.™
Used by permission. All rights reserved worldwide.

A catalogue record for this book is available from the National Library of Australia

ISBN 978 0 7022 6299 9 (pbk)
ISBN 978 0 7022 6451 1 (epdf)

University of Queensland Press uses papers that are natural, renewable and recyclable products made from wood grown in well-managed forests and other controlled sources. The logging and manufacturing processes conform to the environmental regulations of the country of origin.

For Bianca, Cooper, Stella and Asher

*They feel but the pain of their own bodies
and mourn only for themselves.*

—Job 14:22

≠

When a killer strikes and slopes
away, what then does he do? When
he
subsides, does he cover his tracks? No,
he leaves his silt on floor and furniture,
walks
contented down the hall: absolved, self-redeemed.
I'm the authority on that. I can tell you he turns—seeps
away.

I

1

≠

Found by a cadaver dog, and yet not
dead. I am left for dead, left to bubble and
peel.
Cadaver dog sniffs me, licks my eye. Then,
as if turning up her nose at a meal, doubles
back.
Perhaps she knows I was merely discarded—an offering
for the surge. The lengths men take to capitalise on natural
disaster.

≠

Autolysis. That's what she's sniffing out.
Some innate ability to seek out the reek of a
cell's
deconstruction. The odour of cytoplasm self-digesting.
She's charged herself with it. She's off her leash. She's
sleek
and possessed. Alsatians, they say, have noses keen like
virgins, temperaments like the scholarly. It's in their
design.

≠

Sable lady. Flecks of tan for adornment.
Demure, or faking it. She rounds the house,
her
jowls quivering with the hurry of the task,
her neck bowing from the withers, all her wit and
senses
casting her round the house again. Necrosis on her mind;
it draws her in. I watch from the mud-caked yard. I watch her
obey.

≠

She paws at the door; gently first,
nosing it, too, like sponging a spill, then
the
urgency grows. She flashes me glances. Quick
stabbing stares likes she's wary of me. *Was it a
murder?*
I see it cross her mind, like it's a mandatory question
she asks on every job. Scratching now, she queries, *Was it
suicide?*

≠

The door is bolted shut. I locked it days
ago. I've been camping on the deck. Been
prey
for the mosquitoes. Since the surge, I've been
seething. Been plotting or charting. Been blue
or
black. It's a process. The way a bruise implies trauma
at the scene, then the capillaries brown. And what of the
perpetrator?

≠

To offer something of my plight, without
the tedium, would be to say I'm alive. To offer
much
more would only serve the voyeur, the delighter—those
who trawl the news for cataclysm. Those who pore archives
for
gore and bloated bodies, and say *pity their souls* while they gulp and
refresh their feeds. Those to whom floods are paltry, and less is never
more.

≠

And yet, events cannot evolve into story
without their retelling, nor oats into gruel
without
water. So think of the mud as porridge, my yard
as the bowl, the slope behind, just as it is, the house—
the
swollen Paddle-Pop shack it's become—as a dwelling-cum-
deathtrap. Then think, why the cadaver dog. Why the story—its
retelling.

2

≠

Let me take you, by boat, back five days,
when the walls of my house were dry, when
murder
was a dark thought the clouds had dwelt on,
but not acted out. When the Great Dividing Range
was
sodden, yes, but retaining her resolve, doing her best to
swallow the downpours. A pent-up rage in the sky. More rain
forecast.

≠

Year's end, and La Niña, *the little girl*,
from '74 had brought gifts, as a doting aunty
does.
In lieu of socks and jocks, she'd come with clouds
she couldn't wrangle into cellophane. Cumulonimbus;
thunder-
heads drunk with Christmas cheer and some say petulance,
their mood grinch-darkened, their thunder spouting off like a
brag.

≠

The clouds held get-togethers all over
the Downs, pissing up and pissing down,
ushering
in the new year, throwing back to '74. They
emptied out in the catchments and the creeks,
relieving
their bladders over the suburbs of the *provincial city*.
The dams were pudgy. The sewers over town suffered
water-cure.

≠

Hair of the dog for the clouds
and populous alike; an intemperance
for
the ages. The sky a full ombre. Troughs,
latrines, gutters agush. An inland tsunami,
still-
born of misadventure and not hate—umbilical,
not biblical. Waters broke, but nothing broke the
waters.

≠

It was black tar, but faster. It flung cars
and swallowed them, their boots gulping
the
air like Goya's dog. It spared other cars. It
rendered them merely vehicles by which the
stories
could travel back to bars and dinner tables. It drew
the fretters; drew gapers to the main street: the town's
artery.

≠

Diners leered over their steaks as swift-water
crews girdled their waists and waded out in the
surge,
wrenching against the current. The moving water
more suasion than force. The junction a carrefour
of
bedlam: the headlong vehicles, their petrified drivers
stamping on the brakes. The useless anchors. The doomed
vessels.

≠

The *cordillera*, the rope of mountains once
risen above the sea, had all but plunged into it.
Those
of the upland thought as much. Their streets awash
with the catchment's failings, their camphor laurels
wading
in hip boots, their fauna clinging to the boughs. Truth is, it
was just a basin, a sink. A few dead, yes. But the rest, merely
bathers.

≠

Before the escarpment's edge is a plateau,
a table, and we of the Valley—the lowly
of
the foothills and plains—are beneficiaries;
getters of that which falls from above. Come
the
surge; the surfeit, bursting through the sluices, through
ephemeral veins like creeks. Down to the homes of the
lowland.

3

≠

Alluvium comes in the aftermath; a silt
one stoops to take a pinch of—kneeling
in
your dining room, amid ruin, working the grit
between thumb and finger—wondering, what of
the
preamble. What panic, or what calm. Was it bravery,
or its antithesis. Kneeling, still, one thinks, what of the
before.

≠

In the before, a man might stand rigid in
his house, not unlike a mast, unmoved by
the
draught of his hallway, feet from where his
children sleep; for whom, he swears, he'd die.
Hollow
proclamations like these are uttered in the before,
when feet are dry. Yet, when waters rise, what of the
resolve.

≠

Resolve. Weak as it sounds. A word
too easily spoken without unclenching
the
jaw, no hard palate to give it any steel. No
need to discern if a man has resolve; he'll soon
tell
you, spout it around until no-one doesn't know.
A man with soft hands, a dry mouth and a tall
tale.

≠

A tale of valour, usually. Past braveries
with pinches of truth. If not complete
fabrications
then orchestrations: perp becomes protagonist;
the arsonist, back from the forest, taking up his post
on
the fire crew. A man standing in his hallway, not unlike
a mast. A man who's not the only one with the benefit of
reflection.

4

≠

From our verandah, we could see
the stilted houses strewn among the
foothills—
set back sensibly from the creek—each
bearing a yellow hue, duller than usual for the
pouring
rain, as if the Great Range was swamping us all.
The yellow hues duller still, overcome by slews of
mud.

≠

We'd seen the evening news—chaos
uptown on the ridge—and wondered when
the
excess might spill over its lip, forced up-
ward and over like some New-Age magma. *The
old
geologies*—acts of God, or the devil incarnate.
A giant extinct. Or just an old mount with a Vesuvian
gripe.

≠

It's easy to think of decimation. Transient
thoughts that come out of nowhere. Thoughts
that
cause a catch in your throat, when there is calm,
and threat is nil. But they go, mostly, when you rattle
your
head. Later, as if beneath a dropper, your brain suffers
the acid of another. Funny how, when trouble's prone, we
scoff.

≠

This is when our guard is down. Denial:
the great muter, the deadener of one's
sense
of danger. We carry on with routine, turn
our backs to the mountain, hurry our kids to
pre-
bed chores; the rain never ceasing, pooling on the
upland and glutting the creeks. Our minds numb to
caution.

≠

The account will be quick
as water. It is hard to retell
without
simile. If I gloss too quickly,
I am sorry. I do not want to linger.
The
details are little plagues to avoid, so
there's that. And hard to retell without
metaphor.

5

≠

Rush is not the word. Not gush or grumble.
I'll settle on guffaw. It was laughter. Cascading,
eerie
laughter. We'd tucked our kids into bed, told them
stories of the big dry. That's a lie; we were ignorant.
Bedtime
was for fairytales, parables and lore from other lands. The
Range—the tickled, thirsty ogre—spitting from his mouth in
guffaws.

≠

Eruption in the sky. A rousing applause.
An ovation the bowing trees were loath to
receive.
The kids were down. Just another riot they'd sleep
through. The power blacked out. We collected each
a
torch and split ways to inspect: he to the back deck, me
to the front. I saw it coming across the yard. The unwanted
visitor.

≠

The yard filled like a theatre—congregation of
dirty water. The show would begin: uprising and
orchestral.
The percussive overture of snares and cymbals on the
roofing iron, the brass, the strings and woodwinds: the
music
of disaster. The conductor, their father—his prompt evacuation,
baton in hand. Tucked his balls inside their shell. Claimed, *Not my
score.*

≠

The water rushed beneath the floor.
I heard it bashing the stumps. I heard
the
car start up the hill in the garage. I heard
its door slam, then slam again. I heard him
coming
back, trudging through mud. I saw his face through
the haze. Saw vespers on his lips. Then, his vanishing
back.

≠

I heard the engine. Saw headlights scarper
on the hill. Lightning's grating flint lit the
sky,
giving intermittent glimpses of the scene:
a torrent plaguing the yard, toys and swings
adrift;
the house a raft. The timber floor became a colander.
Seepage turned to flush in seconds. The sky followed me
inside.

≠

There are better words than
surreal for how it feels to be
oceaned,
when, moments before, the safety
of houses was surety. Sloshing the
hall
to their doors, I halted, my hands in
arrest. The water tonguing my shins like
eels.

≠

An ear to their doors, I strained to hear
them stirring. Why I didn't burst in I won't
say.
It pains me to think what we're incapable of
in the coldness of the moment. I backed away,
thinking
better to leave them unaware of the torrent, the
creek climbing the walls. Unaware I considered
escape.

≠

But I stayed. Reason told me as much.
Said it'd pass. Said the clean-up would
be
hell, though worth it for the breath in our
lungs. The things you decide in a black out,
when
the floor's immersed and all is awash: to wade
it out. To grit teeth against probability—remain
present.

≠

I stood at the kitchen bench,
motionless, water rising knee-
high.
It began to swirl round the dining
room, floating furniture. A deranged
killer
dancing, his hands rising to my waist.
I was static in his grasp, stunned as warm
prey.

≠

What to do but cross my chest,
for it rose there next. All were lost
at
this height, and hope, too. The torrent
grew fiercer, barging windows, shifting
walls,
testing the stilts. I climbed the bench. Bought
a minute, stretching the rise, my head at the wall's
verge.

≠

Oh quiver and quandary, it rose to my chin.
The filthy prick licked at the cornice, like tasting
its
own shit, and *Fuck!* moaned he, *I didn't rise enough
to take the lot.* Holding on to the pot rack we'd fastened to
the
ceiling, I gasped and wept for my children, thinking better to dive
and die, too. Yet something of my own poltroonery held me from my
end.

≠

No sooner had it arrived than it began
to recede. I was disoriented, estranged
from
my own house, my own body. I floundered
in the dark for a long while, submerging only
to
ram my head against the bench or strike lino. Thought
I'd kicked towards the hall. Arrived only where I'd started
from.

≠

Treading water, feeling for walls,
clues, I tried to gain a bearing. My
feet
began to strike furniture, pedalling,
kicking the dining table, the TV. Came
upon
the couch. Me, the ravaged prey. The killer
creek slaked, sitting me down, feet upon the
ground.

≠

The floorboards were a sick
sieve, draining the stomach bile,
leaving
behind chunks of pea and ham too
big for the cracks. I reclined in a stupor
on
the couch. It gave me a soggy embrace.
A break in the clouds, it seemed, right on
cue.

≠

I gathered myself, slumped down
the muddied hall. It was black. I felt
for
their doors, opened them a crack as if
peeking in to check they hadn't kicked
their
blankets. I called their names, low, and waited
for their lamps to light their little faces, their little
souls.

6

≠

The morning sun was a taunt. I'd spent
the night on the deck. Couldn't stand to be
inside,
couldn't leave and summon help. And what good
was it. At dawn, I searched the kitchen for a knife,
promised
to plunge it in my neck. I found one, ran my thumb across
the blade, testing its ire. Again, I failed them. Drowned in only
dread.

≠

Spent the whole day cursing the sky.
The blue, fucked mass of it. Cirrus
angels—
beatific and wispy—boiling my blood. The
choppers came, cleaving silence. I hid on the deck;
not
ready yet to declare survival, my self-preservation for
the town to exalt. I'd take time. Pick another day to face my
demons.

≠

I walked the boundary to find I was marooned.
A mud island trapped by a bulging creek, flooded
in
on three sides, the Range at the rear. Good. I didn't
want the brigade, nor ambos charging in with gurneys,
the
coppers hounding the place, journos slavering over the story.
The choppers kept at it. But I let the day end, sat on the deck in
darkness.

≠

That night, I swear I heard them crying
in their beds. Bad dreams, calls for water
or
cuddles. Since that night, I didn't dare
venture inside. For dignity, wretched pride,
just
my being their mother. I'd muck out the house
come morning, make their beds, tuck them in with
prayers.

≠

From the deck, I woke the day. I watched it sleep
all night. The mosquitoes haloed my limbs—for the
night
feed: blood offerings. I let them gorge on me. Took
a morning walk, got the jump on the choppers, walked
the
boundary again to ensure my island remained afloat. The creek
was up. The gums along its banks were soldiers—trench-footed,
hyperaware.

≠

The yard like a flipped fritter, or a
topsy-turvy swatch of plush pile, its
inter-
woven roots, stark and reaching to the skies,
like sinners at the altar, but dumb. Me, the inter-
locutor,
squelching through with my boots, inciting a reply,
interrupting the mad silence, muttering their prayers in
relay.

≠

From the yard, the house was on a lean, as though
it took a knee in the mud or jutted its hip in the stance
a teacher assumes before chastising a pupil. And what
was my infraction? Reader, it was supposition. It was my assent
to the fact that the children were dead, without proof. It was
cleaning day. I'd look in on them soon—for confirmation, for
absolution.

≠

I stood there in the front yard, the dank haze of
humidity rising around me like steam from a fresh-laid
dog turd. The fug was contagious. My mind swam.
It, too, a pitiful survivor. Swimming up the footpath to
the deck, pushing the door, heading for the hallway. De-
socketing their doors, it found them: asleep; oblivious to the un-
rest.

≠

It reminded me of Saturday mornings.
Waking late to find them gone from their
beds.
Standing in the hall, unsure if they existed at all;
confusion set off by sleeping outside one's routine.
Can't
tell you I didn't inspect closer. At their bedsides, feeling
for remnant warmth. Body-shaped impressions that can't
lie.

≠

Of course, they were up with the cartoons,
or out in the kitchen, spilling milk. They were
with
their father, bunching leaves. They were some-
where, elsewhere. And yet, the dread of their being
no-
where compelled this scrutiny. One morning he caught
me in my panic. With a smirk, he asked if I'd seen the
children.

≠

Stirring more, he said words
to the effect: *You know, if we
lost
them, it'd be the end of us.* I still
can't be sure if he meant the end of
our
marriage, the botch it was, or the end
of our lives. Either way, we'd lost our
will.

≠

My mind retreated to where I stood.
Through the gloom, the garage came into
focus;
up the hill at the end of the driveway—the
conductor's raised podium. Built on a high enough
elevation
from the house, it'd hardly dipped its ankles. An eyrie
from which he'd spied his ill-fated house and made his
escape.

≠

I scaled the small hill and my stomach turned
at the sight of the floodmark, not even a foot off
the
ground, smeared along the shins of the garage walls
like curse words; scrawled in haste like nasty adolescent
insults
aimed at those of greater, or lesser, fortune than their author—
whose malice is evident by the way they're deposited for another's
interpretation.

≠

I'd come for the garden hose, the wheelbarrow,
a couple of yard bags: means by which I could clear
the
house of its creek mud and clutter. Up a ladder, a musty
windowed attic the children had used as a cubby; an even
better
eyrie from which they would spy the house, plead ignorance
when called for dinner, or bath time, or just for warmth on wintry
days.

≠

I hummed to myself under that attic, just to hear
something other than recollection: their delighted squeals
soaked up in the bones of the place; their shrills the
day they found the python coiled in a corner, the quiet inter-
loper working a whole mischief of rats down her throat. I
collected the supplies, hummed louder still—my own interjection.

≠

There I was at the steps to my house:
a one-man mud army, sleeves rolled up like
the charitable, broom and barrow at the ready.
And what the fuck for? For something to do, get the
mind off things, restore some order to the place, some
domestication. How my body ached. My head a rattled
mess.

≠

The house stank like a licked hand.
The VJ walls, the curtains, the cornices—
the
creek-spoilt—all declaring defeat. Strange to
see the ceiling, untouched and unplagued like a
first-
born Jew on Passover night. To see the space between it
and the floodmark at the cornice: a breathe-space. A saving
grace.

≠

Hadn't eaten since, so I scraped through the silt
and rubble in the kitchen. Found a tin of beans the
water
had moved to the sink. Found a spoon, wiped it clean of
silt, and ate. I stood there in the kitchen, amid all the mud-
spoilt:
the guileless toaster hanged by its cord, the wide-mouthed oven,
the crockery, the tableware—displaced and defaced. All the soiled
domesticity.

≠

The curtains were torrefied strips of hide,
the whitegoods no longer so. The architraves
engorged
gluttons. Oh, the gluttony. The beans were only entree.
Then began a binge: the spam, the spaghetti, corn kernels
and
cream of mushroom; anything with a ring-pull. I walked towards
the hall, peered into it and dry-heaved. Then began a conjuring—a
purging.

≠

I wanted to gouge it from my eyes:
the image, the imagining. Little hands
reaching
through the gap of a door. Crawling the
hall, I lay down on my face, placed my
hand
in the gap, as if to link fingers. There was
nothing there. Only dried mud. Only silt and
apparition.

≠

I sat with my back to their doors, bit down
on my cheeks till bleeding. Through snot and
tears,
I spoke to them, said their names and sang to them.
I told them lies about me, about their father. I told them
floods
were a farce, and inland tsunamis were only fibs we've told for
years to scare them from the creek. *Don't you fret*, I said, *it's all myth.*

≠

I drifted off, and the hall became a corridor
of rainforest, became an aerial walkway from
years
ago in the Daintree, when the kids were still in
nappies and days were a grind, and holidays, in the
scheme
of things, were something within which the grind could
continue somewhere tropical. Fools! We thought we knew
disquietude.

≠

Sorting fact from figment, my mind's eye
twitched. My snores reverbed down the hall,
the
walkway, the canopy of trees. The children ran
ahead, nappies loaded, squealing the happy squeals
suited
more to budgies enjoying their strangulation. Towards us,
wearing suits and ties, walking along the wooden planks: two
men.

≠

The men bent down, picked the
children up. One for each. I tried
to
raise my voice in protest, but it wouldn't
carry. The men, too, held each a tether
which
reached into the sky. Above, two mosquitoes the size of
pterodactyls, with probes like javelins, lifted all to another
realm.

≠

I understood the giant mosquitoes
to be spy blimps or, rather, as flying
hearses.
And the men to be agents, or lawmen.
(Even in a dream, I couldn't accept them as
undertakers.)
True to form, he just stood there—the conductor,
their father—capitulating, planning already, a candlelit
vigil.

≠

I came to in the hall and swatted the air.
The mosquitoes' whining buzz manifested
as
the two-stroke motor of a dinghy, underway on the
swollen creek. It sounded close enough for alarm.
I
knew it'd be a rescue mission. Some band of charity
scouring the banks like ibis, or pterodactyls from a
dream.

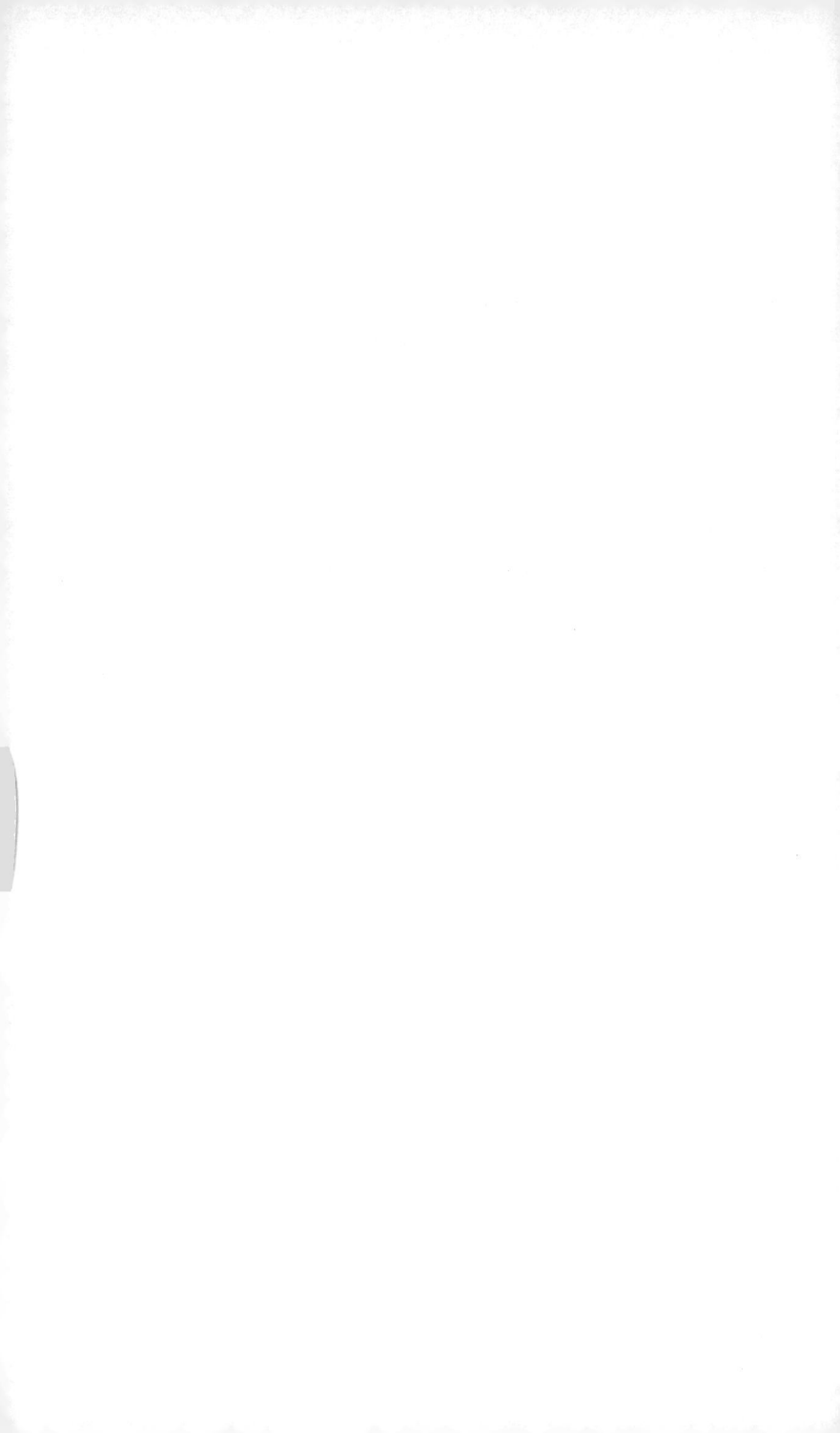

7

≠

The dinghy was coming. A mechanical
reaction: the leaping to my feet, rushing
for
the yard, as though rescue was something I required.
Doubtless something my body desired. It was smarting.
My
stomach roiled in hunger, my joints were gritty, my head, my
fucking head. My ears. The wing-beat of a hearse coming for my
children.

≠

Panic wealed on me like hives. My mind was a
scatter. I hadn't yet cleaned the house, nor had I
bathed
the children. They wouldn't be taken. Not in their
state. And fucked if I'd be put to task for maternal
in-
competence or, worse yet, lauded for my courage. We'd
make the place look empty. We'd go somewhere higher, in
hiding.

≠

I stood at their rooms, my hand on a
doorknob, but it wouldn't turn. Couldn't
muster
the gall, the insolence, the belated chivalry.
And yet pride, of all the poisons, is the one we
guzzle,
despite caution, despite the peril in its consumption,
out of noble intentions and reparation. Out of self-
coaxing.

≠

Macabre, indeed, I concede. Insist,
as you may, that I resort to euphemism,
spare
you vision of their cherubic faces, the expression
upon which they came to settle. And I will, since I did
not
see that for myself. I went in blinded, advancing by feel,
a towel the slouching wreath upon my head, the Lord as my
judge.

≠

Not unlike a cadaver dog myself, really:
suppressing four of the senses to give rise
to
the proficiency of the fifth, my dumb hands
working their rooms, patting shyly the thresholds,
the
rugs, damp and oddly in place, their dressers, stout and
unmoved. Their little selves. Now, how to move them up the
hill.

≠

I'd like to tell you I didn't use the wheelbarrow,
but that would be fabrication. I'd like to diminish
culpability
by stating fact: I'm a grieving mother, not a mortician.
I loaded my babies in, made a way through the sludge of
the
backyard, carved a track any man of small intelligence—by
missing it—would render his position on the rescue squad
redundant.

≠

Quite the task while blindfolded,
so let the towel slip. Took a run up,
surging
ahead—two goes at the hill, parting mud,
driving the wheelbarrow through, reaching
summit.
I hid them in a corner of the carport. Kept my
gaze from them, and turned, peering down from my
eyrie.

≠

Took up the old canvas he'd pulled
from the car before his abscondence,
swept
the crusher dust of the carport with my
foot, concealing, at least, that little trek,
and
laid the canvas over them. Then I listened.
The dinghy was near. We were the swept
away.

≠

I scaled the ladder to the attic. Silver-
fish freaked and swam in squiggles through
dust.
I crawled through the wiring of cobwebs, trying
not to think about pythons, trying to ignore the stench
of
rat piss, their staled droppings. I knelt in a pinch of light.
The window framed a scene: mud-carpeted ruin, not from
memory.

≠

The dinghy materialised at the boundary,
its orange rude against the yard. From it,
ungodly
tones: a man's voice calling for his children; the
conductor come to lend a hand. I sat, seething in
silence.
Could've busted the window, thrown curses like shards
of glass. I shifted to crouching, thinking: lunge or bide my
time.

≠

I watched them step ashore.
A posse formed of volunteers—
neighbourhood
watch from up the creek—slow-talking
men with more teeth in their heads than
brain
cells. The rest were SES. From their stance and
slow gait, I could tell they were duds. Men he could
trust.

≠

The thrill of hide-and-seek. The scree of a galah
in the gums, offering my position. The conductor—
pacing,
stubbled and frenetic, mimicking the bird, calling our
names as if we might fall from somewhere. He and his
men
searching first the yard, then he sent them trundling through
the house, the timber floors reporting their progress. He kept
outside.

≠

He stepped around the house,
leaning, pressing his hands against it,
as
though keeping it upright, or pushing it askew.
With an ear to the weatherboards, he stilled. He
was
listening for the find. No spine. Had a mind to rush
him, collect a shovel on my way. That, he'd have least
expected.

≠

He became the supplicant—hands together
for mercy and miracle, feet apart in the mud,
laconic
in his prayer, rehearsed in proper response
to the unsavoury, the unsettling, unlearning the
mnemonics—
swapped the *Save Our Souls* for *Rest In Peace*,
skipped the *Stay Around and Fucking Drown*—
pathetic.

≠

The back door delivered men
delivering news: no souls inside.
No-
one. No bodies; no shit. He seemed to
stagger forward then catch himself. Word-
less
and smacked, he straightened. Walked himself
onto the deck. He'd take his own tour to make
certain.

≠

While he was in the house, the others
loitered like councilmen, until one looked
down,
followed the wheelbarrow track with his eyes.
I saw what he saw: mud, goaded to part way
for
a snake or a soul not wanting to be found. I'd been
a python, a rat-sized lump in my throat, goading
mud.

≠

At the collective turning of heads, their
gawking up to where I hid, my fear was
of
odour. Did my children smell. Day three,
midsummer, had their bodies yet surrendered.
Fearing:
was I immune to it, the putrescent seeping-away.
Was it already customary, swathing in the scent of
disassembly.

≠

Stepping closer, query sewn to
their faces. Then he appeared,
came
up at the rear, shouldered through
his men, laid eyes on the trench. From
the
attic window, I spied his face as he slowly
cottoned on. His mouth formed the shapes of a
lie.

≠

Thieves! he declared, spitting the lie
into being. *Bloody thieves!* He advanced
at
pace so as to leave the men where they stood.
Turning back to address them from afar, he put
it
to them that he'd been robbed, that some low-life
prick had looted the place. *Not again*, he cried, *not
again!*

≠

Entering the carport, he slowed, speaking
loudly to discourage approach from the men.
Heard
him rummage through tools on the workbench,
clicking his tongue, murmuring nonsense neither I
nor
the men could make out. He listed off items we'd never
owned. *All gone*, he declared. His voice cracked. *Gone*, he
repeated.

≠

He'd have sensed we were there. He'd have
seen the canvas. He'd have noticed its odd re-
location,
its crumpled mound. If there was odour, he'd have
registered it. I remained fixed at the window. His men,
by
not breaking from their huddle, had given countenance to his
fable. I wonder if then—feet away—the children registered *his*
presence.

≠

I watched the party subside, retreat
to search again the yard and boundary.
The
conductor remained. I couldn't catch a breath.
I lay down, pressed an ear to the attic floor. My
hand—
resting palm up—closed into a fist, levitated an inch,
extruded a knuckle, and knocked twice. The drop of a
grenade.

≠

Lord bless him, he spoke my name.
I heard the quick shuffle of his feet,
saw
the ladder with the weight of his body,
ascending rung by rung, delivering him
into
view. Took a second for his eyes to adjust.
When he registered me, his face fell white as
bone.

≠

A wordless exchange. His eyes,
frightened as children, recoiled. I got
to
my knees, clawed hands on the floor, and
hissed like a demon. He yelped, releasing the
ladder,
descending like Beelzebub. Devils, both of us.
One a mother. One a child. The others, not too far
away.

≠

A voice in my head said, *Pity not*,
so I scurried to the top rung, hissed
again
at the fool writhing in the dust, clutching
his knee, his back. I was a fiend, hung like
a
bat, teeth bared. He got up, hobbling in escape,
rounding up his men, calling elsewhere the
search.

≠

Downstream, I heard
him call. Something of
collection,
of gush and force. The men
abandoned their token look-
see,
nodding; shoulders to the dinghy,
mud sucking their feet, their eyes
downstream.

II

8

≠

It's been one day since the dinghy. Five days
since the surge. One night since the shifting: the
tectonic
displacement of a feeble mind; the return of children
to their resting. Sucked it up this time. Didn't contem-
plate.
I looked into their faces. Let go of their blood. Let my blood
rest within them. Tucked them into bed. Shut their doors against
disruption.

≠

When turning from their rooms,
my feet pick up, wary of toys and
building
blocks, the spiteful edges they possess.
I'd trade that pain for the kind I feel now.
Pain
of the clicking latch in my ears. Closed doors
asserting finality. The hall, an eyewitness, building
tolerance.

≠

More than just a corridor,
the hall had been a runway,
a
pirate's gangway. Tunnel for
escapees. The make-believe of
child's
play. In effect, halls are a breeze-
way, mere conduits for those with no
imagination.

≠

Draughty houses like this are a thoroughfare
for wayward spirits and good angels alike. The
cracks
and unsealed entryways are invitations—come if
your composition allows, breathe yourself in through
gaps
in the floor, bear witness to the mortal method of existence,
the way we live on this side. But do not stay. There are none
alike.

≠

Only me, the bloodless wraith,
drifting down the hall, my children
in
their beds. I tiptoe, lest the floorboards
rouse them. I paw the kitchen bench for
the
knife, head for the door. I'll leave the house
to the spirits. To the draught I'll leave the
hall.

≠

Knifing the air, I pull the front door,
step onto the deck, teeth the blade, a
flash
of metal reflecting in the window. I peer
through glass like he'd have done, bereft
of
bottle and balls. The blade snickers, just as
much spite as me. It tongues for me. I see the
black.

≠

With the knife, I pace the deck.
I decide it'll be my neck. There
will
be an audience: gums, galahs, the
crows if they like. Won't do it at
the
house. I'll go to the creek, make them
search. Muster the mettle; plunge cold
steel.

≠

Again, I see black. Perhaps it's just
a floater, a fleck in the periphery. Perhaps
a
beast come to take me to its lair. *Knock your-
self out, but hide me well.* For a trade it could
guard
the place, finish any man who puts a paw on this door.
The black is no fiend, no shadow throwing shadow, no spirit
dog.

≠

The black is not figment. It swims
in sable. The splendorous mix.
Cadaver
dog, free of her handler, come to witness
my clocking off. She might force the blade.
Dog
of revelation, her declaration's certitude: *I have
found that which putrefies, those who reach the end of
days.*

≠

The creek's receded, having pillaged
enough. El Niño will follow, plotting
exsiccation.
Choppers have let up for dogs on the ground.
Now there's a way in by foot—a quick-mud way
in.
Cadaver dog light-footed it, floated in on a whim or
an axiom; where there was death, there is stench and
opportunity.

≠

I stagger to the yard. She trails me,
keening my intent. She's eyes for the
knife.
She ignores the calls of her handler, who's
lost her. Though distant, I hear alarm in
the
voice. It fades. It's just me and her. Our like-
ness already apparent. We're both here for the
solve.

≠

Does she think she'll thwart the plan,
standing like a decree. More hold on the
Earth
than me—my two-legged uprightness. A
little easterly blow would bowl me over. She
tilts
her head. The universal gesture for *what the fuck*.
Her glare makes me giddy. I take a knee. She comes
forward.

≠

Though the urge to draw away
must be torture, she sits with me.
She
affords me her profile. She's regal.
A silky, dark lass. Her warm breath
moves
something in me. I force the knife into the
mud. We both flinch. She glares at it, then
me.

≠

She and I watch the blade as if it
might uproot itself and hop like an
escapee,
legs bound. But I've moved past escape
from the children's father. Indeed, that's
what
I'm telling myself. Equally urgent, we lunge for
the knife. She's quicker than death, and off. The
escapee.

≠

She didn't come down in the last shower.
Perhaps not the time for puns, but she knows
knives,
knows their sole purpose, the ensuing rot of the
result. She's helped decommission a few in her time—
found
them lodged in sinew, or dumped in haste within meagre
vicinity from a shallow grave. Far from the forger's vice and
stained.

≠

Disarmed, I don't give chase. Cadaver dog
trots—prances, rather—to the boundary fence
to
conceal the knife beyond it. Now it's about remains.
She must obey the pull more possessive than gravity.
Think:
the step into a walk-in robe—the summer death of a rodent,
the eviction of all the cupboard's innards. A forgotten shoe the
crypt.

≠

The challenge seems not to be in coming
within range of rotting flesh. She's got her
basis.
Though vicinity's too broad a term, in the
way murder and forethought curl up together
under
the one sweaty blanket. The challenge is in pulling
up a corner, rolling it to the spot, sitting there, surely
pinned.

≠

Cheap thrills, sitting here the beholder,
officiating from the yard. Many nooks have
the
Queenslander, many spaces above and around,
a void like a throat below. I watch her tack about,
sleuthing
like the first on the scene. She clambers up to the deck,
sniffing at a window, fogging the glass, peering in like a
detective.

≠

The space beneath the floor is a cavern: a
retreat for the fauna of the Valley; a shady
haven
for rat and possum and fox, for bulbous tick
and bandicoot, for ant of colours: white, and of
black
and of fire. Now, since the surge, it's a tomb, fenced
by timber slats, where odours from the creature deaths
amass.

≠

It's underneath for her now. The odour
molecules skitter on the air, arousing the
receptors
of her nose, pulling her round as if steered
by a bit. She enters the subfloor through the
open
hatch where my children do not rest. They're
up in their beds. But there are many gaps in the
floor.

≠

Imagine her now in the subfloor of the house—
darting between the timber piers like a pinball, senses
pinging,
reeling her round, drawing nearer the children, edging ever
closer, trying to suppress the *parti pris*. The one that points to
me—
the murderous bitch—the one whose survival reeks of grievance,
not grief, whose melancholy counterfeits as the doldrums, faked and
guilt-ridden.

≠

I come to the house, fold to my knees,
peer into the darkness of the subfloor, my
sight
green with the sudden contrast of light. She's on
hind legs, reaching for the floorboards, licking their
under-
side. She's positioned adjacent to the hallway. There's
a catch in my throat. She's under their rooms, turning hyper-
active.

9

≠

Kneeling and glaring into the scene,
my mind floats away to salvage and re-
collect:
a winter night—drier times, hard in their
own way. We and the walls, huddled round
the
hearth. The kids bathed and smelling of milk.
The blocks of ironbark smelting like ingots of
gold.

≠

We'd traded off, as parents of toddlers
do. He'd wrestle them into bed if I'd take out
our
rubbish for collection day and get more wood for
the night burn. A domestic scene—prosaic and of the
first
world. And a fair trade, since both tasks involved elements of
dread: toddlers, like terrorists, are inexorable, and the wood wasn't
cut.

≠

The night air stung. Took
a torch to guide the way. It
offered
a sickish, yellow light, towards
which I pulled the wheelie bin
laden
with nappies, loose waste. A plume
laid in wake. Otherwise, the night was
black.

≠

The house on reapproach was like
an owl sitting squat in the dark, windows
lit
like eyes trickle-charged through the day,
emitting strange sounds from—where: the belly,
the
throat, perhaps. The mouth remained closed. I was like
a prowler, keeping to the shadows, thinking of pulling the
fuse.

≠

To have placed a cheek against
the weatherboards that night, I may
have
felt the warmth from the hearth, as I do
now, beaming to the outer skin—floors
and
knocking knees of the place, now weeping sweat—
the chatter inside, the bedtime squeals. Memories to
hold.

≠

We kept the woodpile in the subfloor,
up on bricks to stave off termites, a few
feet
in to keep it dry. One had to stoop to avoid
the floor joists, curve the spine and advance
like
the afflicted. I found the woodpile dwindled to
splinters. Above, little feet ran the hall like heavy
hooves.

≠

I didn't bother cutting wood that night.
Instead, I eavesdropped. I sat in the circle
of
torchlight, my back to the base of the fireplace
for what little warmth it offered, and listened to
their
small voices, their bedtime chatter about the day, their
father's low voice willing them to sleep, their pleas, their
innocence.

≠

You could say it was a little weird—
crouched in the sinful cold of a winter
night,
beneath the timber floor like a starving rat,
listening to a private conversation. But who
has
not stood outside a child's door and smiled at their
interaction, the things they say when they think you're
gone.

≠

I stoop like I did that night.
My eyes adjust. Genuflecting, I
advance
on all fours, for ease and sacrosanctity,
approach the bluestone fireplace, stop
and
place a hand to feel it warm with summer and
dying winter coals. Cadaver dog cocks her head,
contemplating.

≠

Common practice for her now to look
for her handler, sit with a nervous twitch
and
wait for her reward. She looks about, but it's
me she sees, my eyes still blank to the scene.
The
low growl from her mouth as she glares at me. Something in the sound of it: the throaty pitch; the accusatory
tone.

≠

My senses heighten: the cold mud beneath
my knees and palms; pining for sunlight, my vision
enhanced, homing in on borer holes and white-
ant stalagmites, cadaver dog in the blurry outer; the sound
of yowls she's working to stifle, the whir of blowflies,
the muffled voices of my children, deadened by sense of smell.

10

≠

They say smell's an inciter. They say deep in
the temporal lobe, snug and reclined, lives the
hippocampus:
an organ—horn-shaped memory cell. Reactor to
smell. A bug. A brain-slug—feeding on moments,
tasting
for momentousness, rating them based on probability,
propensity: are they likely to return and, if so, what will be
triggered.

≠

For me, it is wrath. For me, the dog
is a dog with the head of a man. The
man
is not growling but clearing his throat,
trying to speak. His eyes are those of a
wolf—
estranged from the pack, from his quartet.
My children's father: the dog with the head of a
man.

≠

The dog with the head of a
man revels in the cloud of flies,
snapping
playfully as they cluster under the
nose, a jeering smile stretching wet
jowls,
a sheen of saliva hung from the hungry glands;
my animus reflected in the animal eye, promising
retribution.

≠

I stumble into fresh air, rage broiling
inside me, leaving the dog to bask in her
accomplishment.
She's found them, and she's stupid-happy
about it. I'm headed for the boundary. I'll
search
for the knife; I'll conceal it, take it to her. In
a cloud of flies and odour, I'll plunge it in her
heart.

11

≠

The russet buffel grass,
sodden but a week ago, now
sun-spoilt—
the chastened, ill-profiting clumps.
My face, nosing among it, searching
for
the blade. Even here, there's a scent spurring
recollection. Sheaves of the stuff bundled for
recall.

≠

Scritta paper: its biblical thinness,
but, oh, the strength in numbers, the
weight
of scripture. That's the smell I smell.
On my belly, beyond the boundary, nose
in
the chapters of Job, between Esther and the
Psalms. The *shunner of evil*. Alas, a sucker for
punishment.

≠

There it lies, taunting silver like Job's
temptation. But cursing God gets you no-
where
quickly. Better to take the knife and run, in
one swift movement, which I do. It's come natur-
ally,
this spitefulness, and I hope it's less self-serving than
atonement, that it's something of a loyal friend, faithful as
arms.

≠

Wishing I was fettered to the boundary fence,
so that in my lunge I'd swipe the air. Regret is
more
a bastard when you feel it before the act. And yet
the act is romantic when played back in your mind;
the
fizz of vengeance tightening your neck's sinews.
Justification urging the conscience to think before you
act.

≠

Without the benefit of Job's council—
three men, robed and wizened, by his
feet—
I make for the house, my hands meeting round
the knife like a tryst, saliva pooling in the culverts
of
my mouth, drowning bywords for revenge. The rationale drowns, too. This, an ongoing theme. Time now for fire.

12

≠

The counting of steps. The twinging of ankles
like unparented twigs, pulled away green in the
violence
of moving water. Like a torrent, I home in on the house.
A flint. A makeshift spark, and *woof*. But will it burn with
the
creek still swelling her up: this house, the octogenarian, beaten
by decades of drought, beggared by a weekend of cloud-glut and
bursting.

≠

But I am getting ahead of myself. And no
need for suspense. No bother with the build-
up.
Better to have it done, do the dog in and watch
her writhe in the bloodied mud. Small consolation,
the
death of a messenger. The delight in the shifting of blame.
The dog's *bewilderment, protein-enriched*. High time to up the
ante.

≠

Must the dog be put to death or sent away with
a beating. It's six of one. Yet, we must do what
must
be done. Hold a child over a basin—virus twisting
the gut, foot soles hovering—or leave them to spew
on
their bedding. A wild attempt at a parallel, I concede.
Yet, in one there is savagery; in the other, sense; in either,
principle.

≠

Gripping the knife, I pray against slippage.
The many palms of history sectioned in the
act.
There she lies, belly-up in the mud, bicycle-
swiping the air. I question her intelligence.
When
I kneel, her tongue lolls in her mouth, tasting my
presence. The knife is unsheathed, waiting to be
summoned.

≠

Setting eyes on something one
desires is a decision made. Volition—
be
it of virtue or depravity—can be a pillar.
When the desire is for the death of another,
or
just a beating and maiming, spite and lust share
a bed. The question afterwards: had I been, or did I
become?

≠

The sun is plunging like it does this side
of the Great Range, like a cigarette tossed
into
water. Enough light from drowning embers
to make out my surrounds. I move closer to
the
dog. I sense her sense me. Odour clouts me. I taste
copper in my mouth. Lie down by the dog, in the kill
zone.

≠

She doesn't move
or make a sound. She's
catatonic.
I reach out, move my hand
to her muzzle, feeling for the
warmth
of her breath, contemplating the
ease of smotheration. Indeed, less
humane.

≠

Instead, I bury my nose into her
coat, the bristles at her shoulder,
warding
off the odour. A moment of affection,
it would seem. But avoidance turns
away,
and disseverance guards myself. Moving
memories into tenements, and dimming the
lights.

13

≠

I am thankful for the half-light.
The dog can feel my hand stroking
her
flank, my fingers palpating her ribs.
Yet, she's blind to it, and slugged on
the
odour—has not sensed the knife, does
not bear its snarl. She's still warm and
unreproved.

Epilogue

≠

It took a rotting steak to coax her away.
An open freezer hatch of grey meat in vying
phases
of spoilage. In the dark, I re-entered the house,
feeling my way to the kitchen, pulling open the door
of
the freezer, scraping its contents to the floor: a reeking
mound for the dog. I heard her at the door, preening in the
waft.

≠

The knife I left in the subfloor, forced into
the mud like a staking flag; vexed, I should
think,
to be left in situ. Cadaver dog padded the floor,
moist nose hardened to the acridity, doubtless torn
between
duty and hunger, inching forward, bristles flattened. My
aim was to make her doubt. To second-guess. To fool with her
senses.

Notes

This work was written after trauma. Some of it merely witnessed, some of it experienced, and some of it caused. It is set at the base of the Great Dividing Range near Toowoomba, and is loosely based on the 2011 Queensland floods on the Darling Downs during which thirty-three people lost their lives.

Epigraph: The scripture from the Book of Job is from the New International Version of the *Holy Bible*.

Part I: 2: *the little girl* is the English translation for the weather phase La Niña. This stanza is referring to the infamous Queensland floods of 1974.

provincial city is from a Bruce Dawe poem of the same title in his book *Sometimes Gladness: collected poems, 1954–1987* (Longman Cheshire, 1988). His poem is about the city of Toowoomba.

Part I: 4: *The old geologies* and Part II: 12: *But I am getting ahead of myself* and *bewilderment, protein-enriched* are lines from Luke Davies's *Interferon Psalms* (Allen & Unwin, 2011). Reproduced with the kind permission of Allen & Unwin.

Part II: 10: *my animus reflected in the animal eye* is from Joel Deane's *Year of the Wasp* (Hunter Publishers, 2016). Reproduced with the kind permission of Joel Deane.

Part II: 11: *shunner of evil* is from the Book of Job in the New International Version of the *Holy Bible*.

Epilogue: *moist nose hardened to the acridity* is from the LK Holt poem 'Memo' in *Patience, Mutiny* (John Leonard Press, 2014). Reproduced with the kind permission of John Leonard Press.

Acknowledgements

None of the work within has been previously published. However, grateful acknowledgement is made to the editors of the following journals for publishing my other works: *Overland, Verity La, Stilts Journal, Concrescence, Mascara Literary Review* and *Tincture Journal*.

I have been overwhelmed by the support of everyone at UQP as we prepared this book for publication. Aviva Tuffield and team, you made the experience unforgettable. A special mention to Felicity Dunning for your brain, and attention to detail.

To Felicity Plunkett, thank you for gifting me with your utmost care, encouragement and insight. I have been touched by your generous spirit.

To Robbie Coburn, Joel Deane, Lucy Nelson and Simon Cleary, thank you for supporting my work and offering much valued advice and advocacy.

Thank you to Denise Spencer, Jackie Bishop, Brad Morris, the Davison family and the Kelland family. You have each given my work a boost in one form or another, in your own way.

To my beautiful parents, Bob and Lesley, and my siblings, Hayley, Jeremy, Natalie and Ashlee (and your wonderful spouses), thank you for believing in my ability. I love you all.

To my wife, Bianca: this book, and its author, wouldn't be without you.